JEFF GORDON

IN THE COMMUNITY

MATT ANNISS

Britannica
Educational Publishing

IN ASSOCIATION WITH

ROSEN
EDUCATIONAL SERVICES

Published in 2014 by Britannica Educational Publishing (a trademark of Encyclopædia Britannica, Inc.) in association with The Rosen Publishing Group, Inc.
29 East 21st Street, New York, NY 10010

Distributed exclusively by Rosen Publishing.
To see additional Britannica Educational Publishing titles, go to rosenpublishing.com

First Edition

Britannica Educational Publishing
J.E. Luebering: Director, Core Reference Group
Anthony L. Green: Editor, Compton's by Britannica

Rosen Publishing
Hope Lourie Killcoyne: Executive Editor
Jeanne Nagle: Senior Editor
Nelson Sá: Art Director

Library of Congress Cataloging-in-Publication Data

Anniss, Matt.
 Jeff Gordon in the community / Matt Anniss.
     pages cm.—(Making a difference: athletes who are changing the world)
 Includes bibliographical references and index.
 ISBN 978-1-62275-190-7 (library binding)—ISBN 978-1-62275-193-8 (pbk.)—
 ISBN 978-1-62275-194-5 (6-pack)
 1. Gordon, Jeff, 1971—Juvenile literature. 2. Automobile racing drivers—United States—Biography—Juvenile literature. I. Title.
 GV1032.G67A66 2013
 796.72092—dc23
 [B]
                                                                    2013024593

Manufactured in the United States of America

CONTENTS

Jeff Gordon has won more races than any other NASCAR driver. In 2009, he became the first NASCAR driver to collect more than $100 million in prize money.

J eff Gordon is one of the greatest race car drivers the United States has ever seen. Since completing his first National Association for Stock Car Auto Racing (NASCAR) event as a teenager, he has become one of the most familiar faces in the sport.

As of August 2013, Jeff Gordon has won 87 NASCAR races, putting him third on the all-time list of winners. However, it's Jeff's activities off the track, and particularly his work for good causes, that has made him one of the country's best-loved athletes. He is a passionate supporter of children's charities, particularly those that work with youngsters with cancer and other life-threatening illnesses. He runs his own charity, the Jeff Gordon Children's Foundation, and has reportedly donated millions of his dollars to supporting good causes. Jeff's tireless charitable contributions have made a significant difference in countless lives.

CHAPTER 1

THE STORY OF JEFF GORDON

When he was just a year old, Jeff Gordon (born August 4, 1971, in Vallejo, California) was taken to his first stock car race meeting at California's Vallejo Speedway. The visit was arranged by Jeff's stepfather-to-be, John Bickford. For Jeff, the visit began a life-long love of racing cars.

John Bickford encouraged Jeff to take an interest in racing from an early age. When he was four years old, John bought Jeff his first BMX, a bicycle used for dirt track racing. One year later, the five-year-old Jeff became the owner of his first racing car, a tiny version

Jeff began his racing career in midget cars such as the one pictured here (right).

of a midget car, which is a small racing car, known as a "quarter midget."

Almost as soon as Jeff received the car, he began practicing his driving skills every night, completing laps on a local dirt track near his family home in Vallejo.

By the age of six, Jeff was ready to take part in his first race. Two years later, he won his first quarter midget championship, beating a number of older children to take the title. By now it was clear that Jeff was born to race.

STAR STATS

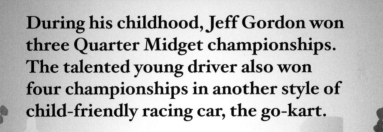

During his childhood, Jeff Gordon won three Quarter Midget championships. The talented young driver also won four championships in another style of child-friendly racing car, the go-kart.

7

MOVING FOR THE DREAM

By the time Jeff was 14, it was clear that he was one of the most talented young drivers in the country. He regularly beat adult racers in quarter midget races, and was keen to step up to full-size midget cars. Jeff even wanted to drive sprint cars, the next level in car racing.

Today, Jeff is one of the most formidable drivers ever seen on a NASCAR track. Here, he takes a moment to prepare for the Gillette Fusion ProGlide 500 race at the Pocono Raceway in Long Pond, Philadelphia, on June 6, 2010.

Jeff's parents knew he had the talent to succeed as a professional race car driver. However, they also knew that very few people ever make it to the top of the sport. They realized that if Jeff was to fulfill his dream, he needed to experience driving adult-size cars against older drivers. So, in 1986, Jeff's parents made the decision to move the family from California to Pittsboro, Indiana, close to Indianapolis, the home of NASCAR racing.

The move turned out to be a wise one. In 1987, at the age of 16, Jeff became the youngest driver ever to be awarded a license to race by the United States Auto Club (USAC).

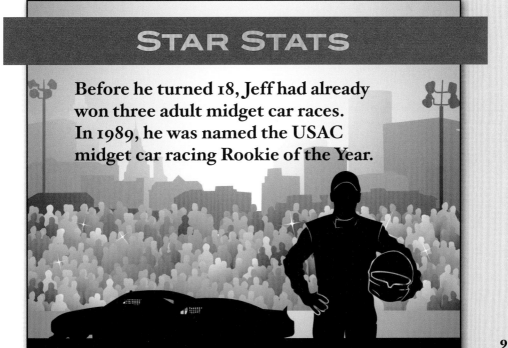

STAR STATS

Before he turned 18, Jeff had already won three adult midget car races. In 1989, he was named the USAC midget car racing Rookie of the Year.

SPRINT CAR RACER

By the time he graduated from high school in 1989, Jeff Gordon had already won more than 100 races. In 1990, less than 12 months after leaving school, he won the USAC National Midget Series.

Jeff was now a full-time professional driver, dividing his time midgets and sprint cars, which are specially built, lightweight race cars. A trip to the Buck Baker Racing school in North Carolina gave him a taste for driving the stock cars used in NASCAR racing. These are faster, modified versions of the cars the general public can buy from dealerships.

STAR STATS

Jeff recorded his first NASCAR Winston Cup Series race win at the 1994 Coca-Cola 600 in Charlotte, North Carolina.

Jeff was nicknamed "wonder boy" by the press for his amazing feats at a young age. Here, the superstar races in his famous Number 24 DuPont Chevrolet in 1997.

Jeff was expected to immediately succeed in NASCAR's equivalent of baseball's minor leagues, the Nationwide Series. However, he struggled and dropped back down to racing sprint cars on the USAC circuit. After winning the 1991 USAC National Silver Crown Series, Jeff returned to the NASCAR circuit in the Winston Cup Series (now called the Sprint Cup Series), the pinnacle of NASCAR racing. The kid they had called "wonder boy" was becoming a man.

NASCAR Champion

When he entered the 1995 Winston Cup Series, Jeff was under pressure. Despite his talent and potential as a future NASCAR great, he had yet to make his mark. The pressure was on.

Throughout the season, Jeff raced against NASCAR legend and seven-time Winston Cup Series champion Dale Earnhardt, Sr. After driving the fastest lap time in qualifying

Jeff holds up his championship cup after winning the Winston Cup Series championship in 1995. The driving superstar achieved the win at just 24 years old!

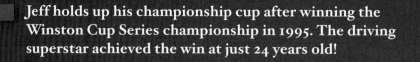

sessions, Jeff started eight races in the pole position, which is the first position at the start of a race. He went on to win seven races, and his first NASCAR Winston Cup Series championship.

It would be the first of many Winston Cup wins for Jeff. He won again in 1997 and 1998, making him the driver to beat on the track. Other drivers dreamed of beating his famous car, the DuPont (Axalta as of 2013) No. 24.

Jeff was now the dominant force in NASCAR motor racing. Along with claiming championships, he was winning the sport's most famous races, including the Daytona 500. He was on his way to superstar status.

STAR STATS

When he won his first Daytona 500 in 1997, Jeff Gordon was just 26 years old. This made him the youngest driver at that time to win the world-famous race.

Jeff takes laps during a NASCAR Sprint Cup track prior to a race in 2011 at Phoenix International Raceway in Avondale, Arizona.

A RACING HERO

The mark of a true sporting great is whether they can turn one or two notable wins into a glittering career. By this measure, Jeff Gordon is one of the greats of auto racing.

In 2001, he claimed his fourth Winston Cup Series championship, putting him fourth on the all-time list of NASCAR championship wins. Only three other drivers have won more championships. Dale Earnhardt, Sr. and

Richard Petty both won seven championships. Jimmie Johnson has won five championships.

In 2013, Jeff Gordon marked his 23rd year of racing in the NASCAR Sprint Cup Series, logging more than 700 starts. Of those, he has finished in the top ten more than 400 times, and won 87 races, making him one of the most successful race car drivers in history.

Since beginning his NASCAR career, Jeff has earned more than $100 million in prize money, and millions more in deals to advertise products. When he stops racing, he will retire as one of the true legends of auto racing.

STAR STATS

In 1998, Jeff Gordon was named one of the 50 Greatest NASCAR Drivers of all time, as part of NASCAR's 50th birthday celebrations.

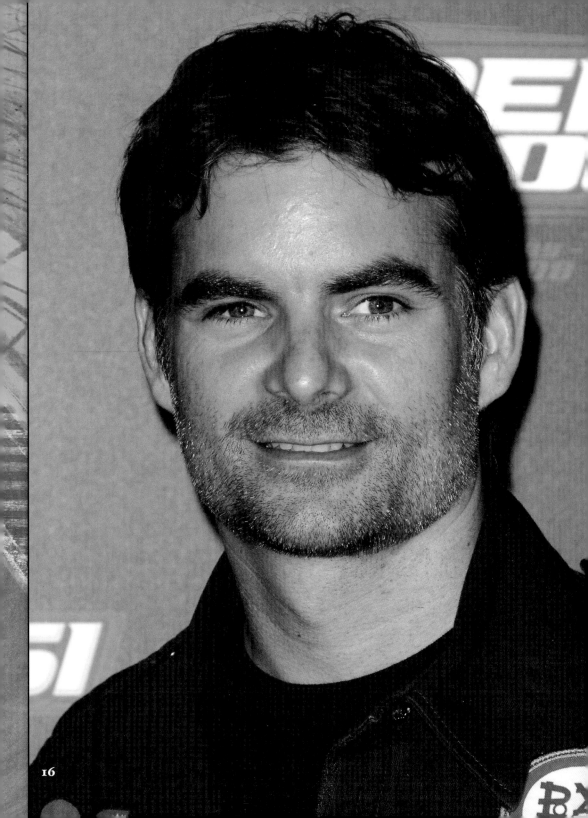

More than a Great Driver

Jeff Gordon's career at the top of motorsport has made him one of the most recognizable athletes in the sport. Even those with little interest in NASCAR racing know his name. They also know the distinctive design of his car, which started out with rainbow colors but has featured a flame (Firestorm) decoration on its side starting in 2009.

Jeff's fame is not a product of his amazing racing career alone. He has also become famous as a supporter of charitable causes. He takes a personal interest in children's charities, in particular the fight against cancer, a deadly disease that kills many young people every year. Jeff has plowed millions of dollars of his own fortune into charities supporting children with cancer, and millions more into research projects to find a cure for the illness.

Jeff is widely considered to be a great role model who has made the most of his talent through hard work. He is an inspiration to others who wish to follow in his footsteps.

Jeff's popularity and fame have led to opportunities for the star beyond the wheel, such as co-hosting the Pepsi 500 Running Wide Open celebrity charity event in 2008.

CHAPTER 2

FOUNDATION
FOR CHANGE

Early in his career, Jeff Gordon began to devote time to charities, including the Leukemia and Lymphoma Society. Leukemia and lymphoma are two forms of cancer, a deadly disease that affects millions of people around the world every year.

Jeff's life changed in 1992 when his good friend, and racing team crewmember, Ray Evernham announced that his son had cancer. Jeff was close to Evernham and wanted to help. He began to volunteer with a number of cancer charities and local children's hospitals.

As he became more involved as a volunteer and charity fundraiser,

One of the most successful NASCAR racers of all time, Jeff uses his sizeable fortune to help people suffering from cancer.

Jeff thought he could make an even greater contribution. He decided to set up his own charity to help children with cancer and other life-threatening diseases, and in 1999, the Jeff Gordon Children's Foundation was born.

In the years since it began, Jeff's charity has helped thousands of people suffering from cancer, and supported their families, too. The foundation has also funded many organizations that are trying to find a cure for cancer.

RAISING MONEY

Jeff has put millions of dollars of his own money into his Children's Foundation. To help raise further funds, Jeff also commits time to fundraising events and charity events.

Every year, the Jeff Gordon Children's Foundation runs a raffle. People buy tickets, and one lucky ticket-holder walks away with a grand prize worth thousands of dollars. In 2013, the grand prize was a brand new Corvette!

STAR STATS

Jeff takes his charity message directly to people's homes by recording television commercials. These are often funded by money from his sponsors, such as Chevrolet, and feature children with cancer, celebrity friends, and other NASCAR drivers.

Jeff's inspirational charity work has inspired others to assist those in need. The organizers of Talladega Superspeedway raised thousands of dollars for charity by holding a Jeff Gordon Day in 2013.

Many other fundraising events take place over the course of the year, including a celebrity bowling tournament and online auctions of rare items from Jeff and other NASCAR racers.

The Foundation also encourages others to try to raise money on the charity's behalf by holding their own fundraising events. In April 2013, Talladega Superspeedway held a Jeff Gordon Day. A percentage of the ticket sales from the day were donated to the Jeff Gordon Children's Foundation.

GIVING BACK

Since its formation in 1999, the Jeff Gordon Children's Foundation has distributed more than $13 million in funding to organizations that work in cancer care or research.

Every year, Jeff meets with the Foundation's directors to decide which organizations will benefit from funding. The money is usually divided among large international projects,

In 2012, Jeff posed for a photograph at Legoland, in Texas, with children battling cancer and their families. The star had spent the morning with children who had benefited from his foundation.

charities that focus on research into cures for cancer, and smaller, localized projects that improve the lives of sick children. Every year, a number of children's hospitals also receive funds to improve the care of their patients.

The Jeff Gordon Children's Foundation directly benefits sick children and their families. In 2012, the Foundation gave $10,000 to a project called Flashes of Hope, which offers families of sick children free family portrait photographs. Additionally, a summer camp in Charlotte, North Carolina, for children with cancer and caregivers at a local children's hospital were each given $15,000.

STAR STATS

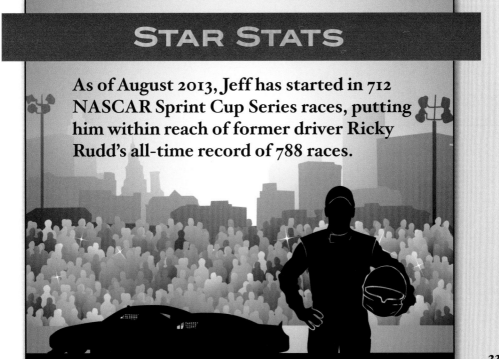

As of August 2013, Jeff has started in 712 NASCAR Sprint Cup Series races, putting him within reach of former driver Ricky Rudd's all-time record of 788 races.

CHAPTER 3

MAKING A DIFFERENCE

As his career has progressed and he has become older, Jeff Gordon has devoted more of his time to charity. Like many other athletes who support community causes, Jeff gives his time for free. The star also makes appearances at events to secure good television and newspaper coverage for the charities that he supports.

To further help the charities he works with, Jeff will often arrange to promote their work through the Jeff Gordon Children's Foundation. For instance, the foundation has encouraged its supporters to raise money for a campaign called Kick-It. The campaign asks people to raise money for cancer

Now a father of a son and a daughter, (Ella, above), Jeff works tirelessly to help raise money to help children suffering from cancer.

24

charities by arranging games of kickball, a version of baseball where players kick the ball instead of batting.

In early 2013, Jeff backed another campaign, called Hats Off to Hope. The project aims to bring joy to children suffering from cancer, using the books and cartoon characters of Dr. Seuss, including the Cat in the Hat. To support the campaign, Jeff wore a specially designed helmet featuring Dr. Seuss characters at the 2013 All-Star race in Charlotte, North Carolina. The helmet was to be auctioned off, with all proceeds from the sale going to the cancer charities supported by Jeff.

STAR STATS

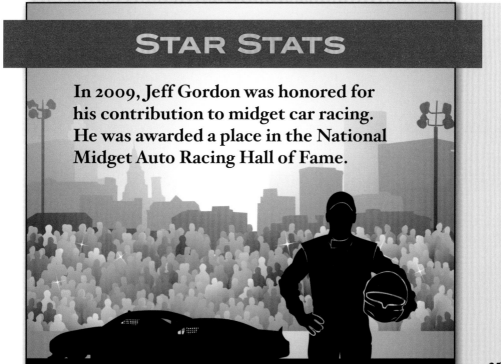

In 2009, Jeff Gordon was honored for his contribution to midget car racing. He was awarded a place in the National Midget Auto Racing Hall of Fame.

Funding Research

One of Jeff Gordon's biggest goals is to help find a cure for cancer. To further this aim, every year his Children's Foundation gives hundreds of thousands of dollars to organizations that fund scientific research into children's cancer.

In 2009, Jeff donated $1.5 million to set up the Jeff Gordon Children's Foundation Pediatric Cancer Research Fund at the Riley Hospital for Children in Indianapolis. The money will be used to fund research into cancer care, with the aim of finding a cure for the deadliest forms of childhood cancer. Some of the funds will be devoted to clinical trials, the testing of possible cancer cures on patients currently suffering from the disease.

Jeff's foundation has also given millions of dollars to other important research projects. In 2012, it gave $176,000 to the Hendrick Marrow Program, which raises money for bone marrow transplants, and $187,000 to the Children's Oncology Group at Nationwide Children's Hospital in Columbus, Ohio.

Jeff Gordon bowls a frame during the Jeff Gordon Foundation Bowling Tournament in 2004. This is just one of the many fundraising events the foundation holds each year to raise money for cancer charities.

THE JEFF GORDON CHILDREN'S HOSPITAL

Jeff Gordon's commitment to helping sick children has been recognized through the naming of a children's hospital in his honor in Concord, North Carolina.

The Jeff Gordon Children's Hospital opened its doors in December 2006 following 18 months of building work. It was paid for by

Jeff stands next to the Sounds of Pertussis Protection Quilt (a square of which he made himself) at its unveiling at the Jeff Gordon Children's Hospital in October 2011.

a combination of Jeff's personal donations, money from the Carolinas Medical Center Northeast, and special fundraising events.

The hospital is designed to offer the best possible care to sick children in the local area. It features a 28-bed pediatric floor, and has its own intensive care unit for children with life-threatening illnesses or injuries. It has state-of-the-art equipment to help those with cancer and serious heart problems, too.

The Jeff Gordon Children's Foundation continues to support the hospital. In 2012, it donated $56,000 to construct a new playground for patients and their families.

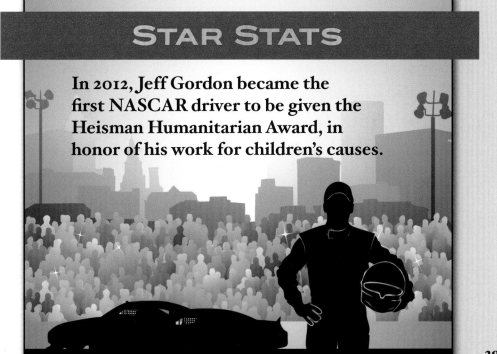

STAR STATS

In 2012, Jeff Gordon became the first NASCAR driver to be given the Heisman Humanitarian Award, in honor of his work for children's causes.

Global Outreach

Although most of the children's cancer care projects funded by the Jeff Gordon Children's Foundation are based in the United States, the charity also funds vital work in East Africa.

In 2011, Jeff announced that the foundation would be donating $1.5 million to a project to bring cancer care to the war-torn country of Rwanda. The NASCAR superstar traveled to Africa in 2011 to see for himself what the money would be used for, including the building of new hospitals. The first cancer care unit in Rwanda, partly paid for by Jeff's donations, opened in 2012.

STAR STATS

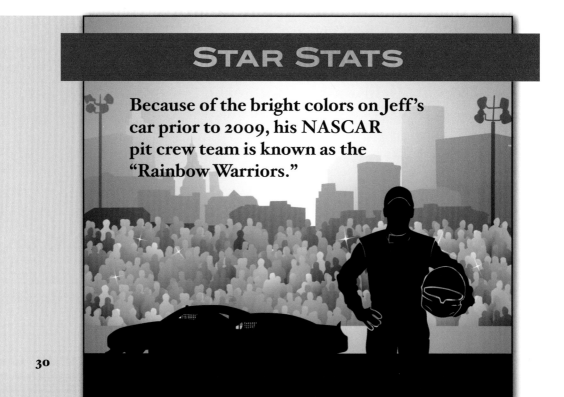

Because of the bright colors on Jeff's car prior to 2009, his NASCAR pit crew team is known as the "Rainbow Warriors."

At the launch of a program to train doctors in Rwanda, Jeff (second from right) poses with former U.S. president Bill Clinton (third from right) and Clinton's daughter, Chelsea (third from left).

Until the Jeff Gordon Children's Foundation became involved, Rwanda did not have a single doctor who specialized in cancer. Jeff is committed to helping eradicate cancer among children in every part of the world. Over the next few years, it is hoped that more Rwandan doctors in hospitals built by Jeff's foundation will be trained in cancer treatment, so that children suffering from the disease will receive the specialist care they need.

ATHLETES FOR HOPE

In 2007, Jeff Gordon got together with many other high profile athletes, including boxing legend Muhammad Ali, former tennis player Andre Agassi, skateboarder Tony Hawk, and Team USA soccer player Mia Hamm to discuss working together to encourage other athletes to become involved with charities.

In May 2007, the group of stars appeared on ABC's *Good Morning America* television show to announce the launch of Athletes for Hope. This is an organization dedicated to connecting both professional and amateur athletes with charities.

Since 2007, more than 2,000 professional athletes have joined the organization and offered their services to hundreds of charities around the world. In 2011 alone, the organization connected athletes with more than 300 different charities, all desperately in need of help and money. All of these athletes became volunteers, and many have also given large sums of money to their chosen charities.

Jeff speaks with the media on October 4, 2012, before meeting children battling cancer who have benefited from his foundation through Speedway Children's Charities.

MAKE-A-WISH

Long before he set up his foundation, Jeff was helping one of the country's most popular charities, the Make-A-Wish Foundation.

This charity is dedicated to granting wishes to children with serious and life-threatening illnesses. Whether children wish to meet a celebrity, ride in a NASCAR car, or play basketball with Kevin Durant, the charity tries to make those wishes come true.

Jeff has made the wishes of many sick children come true by taking them to NASCAR race events. There, children get to watch the superstar race, then hang out with him afterward as he signs autographs for his fans.

Since first offering his services to the Make-A-Wish Foundation in 1995, Jeff Gordon has made over 230 wishes come true. In fact, he's granted so many wishes that the charity has given him a special award.

Many children the charity helps wish to meet Jeff and hang out with him at NASCAR races, but some wishes are different. In 2011, Kentucky teenager Johnathon Ousley asked to go camping and fishing, and meet Jeff. The NASCAR star and the Make-A-Wish Foundation made his dream come true.

STAR STATS

Jeff is among only a handful of athletes and celebrities who have granted more than 200 wishes through the Make-A-Wish Foundation. As of July 2013, World Wrestling Entertainment (WWE) wrestler John Cena held the record, having made an amazing 300 wishes come true.

S portspeople can be great role models for youngsters. This means that their actions on the field, track, or court, and their behavior off it, set a good example to anyone watching. Following a healthy lifestyle, training hard, and being committed to excellence are all examples of great behavior for young people. By watching sportspeople excel, youngsters are likely to be encouraged to try to achieve similar goals.

Jeff is always happy to talk to fans and sign autographs. Here, he addresses fans at the Phoenix International Raceway in Arizona.

Jeff Gordon is widely thought of as a great role model for youngsters. Those who have worked for or driven with him say that he is the perfect teammate, while charities are full of praise for his tireless work for good causes. Jeff is an amazing driver, but he has reached the top of NASCAR racing only through hours of hard work and practice. He could have wasted the millions of dollars he has won in prize money, but instead he has given much of it to charity.

STAR STATS

In 2009, Jeff Gordon was given the Silver Buffalo Award by the Boy Scouts of America in recognition of his charity work for sick children.

A Belief in God

Jeff Gordon is a devout Christian and tries to live his life by the teachings of the Bible. An urge to show kindness and consideration to others has driven Jeff to devote much of his time to charitable causes.

Jeff did not grow up in a faith-filled household. His family didn't go to church, and Jeff only started attending services regularly in 1992. He was inspired to go to church after following other NASCAR drivers to the local chapel one day. As he listened to the service, Jeff began to think about his own faith, and a belief in God grew.

Since then, Jeff has spoken about his belief in God and the importance of faith. He has even said that he believes that God keeps him safe from dangerous car crashes, which occur regularly in the world of NASCAR racing.

"I put a lot of faith in God," Jeff told talk-show host Larry King in 2001. "I've been through some nasty wrecks and have come out with no injuries. So I certainly thank God for that each and every day."

Jeff Gordon with wife Ingrid Vandebosch and their children, Leo and Ella Sofia, in 2011. Family life and his faith are of prime importance to Jeff.

INSPIRING OTHERS

Jeff Gordon's easy-going personality and lack of "celebrity" ego make him an extremely popular character in the sporting world. Off the track, Jeff is quiet, soft-spoken, thoughtful, and willing to help others less fortunate than himself. The sports star also tries to be a great father to his young children, Ella and Leo.

Jeff's feats on the racing track are equally inspirational. He was one of the youngest drivers ever to race in NASCAR when he first joined the circuit in 1990, at 19 years of age. Since then, several drivers, including current

STAR STATS

In 2012, officials in North Carolina announced that a portion of Interstate 85 was to be renamed the Jeff Gordon Expressway, in the star's honor.

Jeff holds up a sign marking the section of the interstate named in his honor. Few stars can claim to be so inspirational that a highway is named after them!

stars Joey Logano and Casey Atwood, have joined NASCAR teams at just 18 years old. Without Jeff's shining example, it is unlikely racing teams would have given these young drivers a chance. Jeff Gordon proved that achieving astonishing success at an early age is possible, if a person is determined to work hard and make the most of his or her talents.

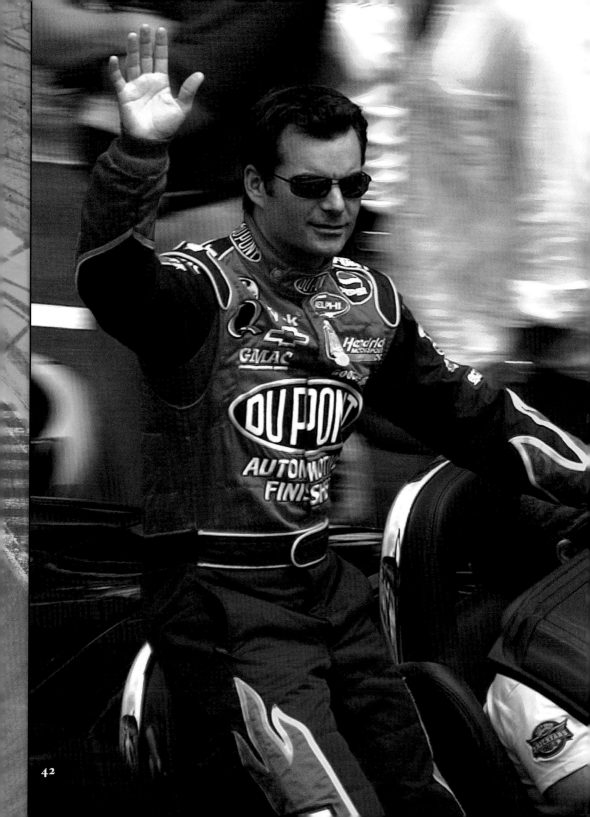

Charity Superstar

Twenty-three years after first driving his famous Number 24 DuPont Chevrolet car in a NASCAR race, Jeff Gordon was showing no signs of nearing retirement. Despite starting more than 700 races, winning more than 80 of those, and becoming a multimillionaire many times over, Jeff still has a thirst for driving racing cars.

The length of his career and his many successes have made him a sporting superstar. He has appeared as a guest on popular television shows such as *The Simpsons* and *Saturday Night Live*.

However, it is probably the star's charity work that makes him such a well-loved athlete. Through the Jeff Gordon Children's Foundation, he has given millions of dollars to improve the lives of many sick children. Thousands more children have benefited from work carried out by charities supported by Jeff. A passionate sportsman and devoted charity campaigner, Jeff Gordon will be remembered forever for his outstanding contributions to both NASCAR racing and his community.

Jeff Gordon's passion for NASCAR racing and his tireless work for charity have made the superstar driver a legend among his peers and fans alike.

TIMELINE OF ACHIEVEMENTS

1976: Jeff steps into a race car for the first time, a quarter midget designed for children.

1977: He records his 35th win in children's races.

1986: To support his dream of becoming a professional race car driver, Jeff's family moves to Pittsboro, Indiana.

1989: He is named USAC Rookie of the Year.

1990: Jeff wins his first significant motor racing championship, the USAC National Midget Series.

1991: He wins the USAC National Silver Crown Series, his second stock car championship in two years.

1992: Jeff wins his first NASCAR Nationwide Series race, the Atlanta 300.

1995: He wins the Winston Cup Series for the first time.

1995: Jeff grants the first of hundreds of wishes for the Make-A-Wish Foundation.

1997: Jeff wins his second Winston Cup Series championship.

1999: He sets up the Jeff Gordon Children's Foundation to help children with life-threatening illnesses.

2006: The Jeff Gordon Children's Hospital opens in Concord, North Carolina.

2007: Jeff joins other athletes to found Athletes for Hope.

2009: He becomes the first NASCAR driver to earn over $100 million in prize money.

2012: The star becomes the first NASCAR driver to win the Heisman Humanitarian Award.

2013: Jeff drives in his 700th consecutive NASCAR Sprint Cup (formerly Winston Cup) Series race, the Bojangles' Southern 500. He finishes third, the 300th time that he's finished a race in the top five.

Kevin Durant
The National Basketball Association (NBA) and Olympic Team USA basketball star has raised money for various charities, including a $1 million donation to the America Red Cross to help victims of the Oklahoma City tornado in 2013.

Robert Griffin III
The pro football player began volunteering for a number of charities while in college.

Mia Hamm
The leading soccer player's Mia Hamm Foundation raises money for families of children suffering from rare diseases.

Tony Hawk
The skateboarding legend's charity, The Tony Hawk Foundation, has provided more than $3.4 million to build 400 skate parks around the United States.

Derek Jeter
The New York Yankees shortstop started his Turn 2 Foundation to support youth programs across the United States.

Magic Johnson
The NBA legend founded the Magic Johnson Foundation in 1991, to fund a range of educational projects. Today, 250,000 young Americans benefit from its funded projects every year.

Peyton and Eli Manning
The record-breaking Super Bowl MVP brothers support many causes through fundraising, including the work of the PeyBack Foundation, the charity set up by Peyton Manning.

Kurt Warner
The former Super Bowl MVP's First Things First Foundation improves the lives of impoverished children.

Venus and Serena Williams
The record-breaking tennis players devote huge amounts of time to charity. They are also fearless campaigners for equal rights for women.

cancer A potentially life-threatening disease.

community A group of people in one particular area.

distinctive Easily recognized, stands out.

dominant To be a controlling force in something.

donate To give to an organization or a charity.

eradicate To get rid of something altogether so that it does not exist any more.

fundraiser A person or event responsible for raising money.

grant To allow something to happen.

inspiration Something or someone that excites and inspires people.

laps Circuits of a motor racing track.

modified Changed or adapted to suit particular needs.

motor racing Any sport that involves racing cars, motorbikes, or trucks.

NASCAR The National Association for Stock Car Auto Racing, the leading motor racing organization in the United States.

oncology A branch of medicine concerned with the study and treatment of tumors.

passionate To have very strong feelings for something or someone.

pediatric Medical care related to babies and children.

pinnacle The peak or highest point of something.

pole position The position close to the start line, given to the driver who has set the fastest time for a lap around the race track in a qualifying session.

potential The hope of future success.

proceeds Monies raised through an event.

promote To encourage an interest in something.

retire To stop performing a role or a job.

role model A person whose good behavior and attitude inspires others.

rookie One who is in his or her first year as a professional athlete.

sponsorship Money paid by a company to support an activity, in return for receiving advertising or promotions.

track A path or road on which cars, motorbikes, or trucks are raced.

BOOKS

Doeden, Matt. *Jeff Gordon* (Blazers). North Mankato, MN: Capstone Press, 2008.

Hoffman, Mary Ann. *Jeff Gordon* (Superstars of NASCAR). New York, NY: Gareth Stevens Publishing, 2010.

Poolos, Jamie. *Jeff Gordon—NASCAR Driver* (Behind the Wheel). New York, NY: Rosen Publishing Group, 2007.

Pristash, Nicole. *Jeff Gordon* (NASCAR Champions). New York, NY: PowerKids Press, 2008.

Sapet, Kerrily. *Jeff Gordon* (Modern Role Models). Broomall, PA: Mason Crest, 2007.

WEBSITES

Due to the changing nature of Internet links, Rosen Publishing has developed an online list of Websites related to the subject of this book. This site is updated regularly. Please use this link to access the list:

http://www.rosenlinks.com/mad/gord